Harmonic Dressage

PART 1

Optimizing Your Seat and Use of the Aids

Gail Hoff, PhD

First Published in the United States of America in 2020
by Los Alamos Dressage Center, 461 Buckboard Lane, Ojai, CA 93023

COPYRIGHT © 2020 by Gail Hoff
All rights Reserved Including the right of reproduction, in whole or in part in any form by any means.

ISBN 978-1-7353111-0-4

Library of Congress Control Number: 2020915984

Illustrations, Book Design and Cover by Daniel Marhuenda Donadeu

Editor: Barbara Christopher

Back Cover Photo: Jan Eisner

Table of Contents

Acknowledgements — **5**

Introduction — **8**

A Word About Dressage — **9**

A Word About the Author — **12**

The Role of the Rider — **17**
- Rider Requirements — **17**
- Independent Seat and Legs — **17**
- The Dressage Seat — **19**
- The Role of the Seat and Legs — **19**
- Upper Body — **20**
- Lower Back — **22**

Co-ordinating the Seat and Legs with the Hands — **25**
- Getting a Horse in Front of he Driving Aids — **25**
- A Word About Delay Time — **27**
- The Role of the Hands — **30**
- The Four Rein Aids — **31**
- Contact and Connection — **33**
- Half Halts — **34**
- Half Halts in the Canter — **37**
- Creating Connection over the Back of the Horse — **38**

Basic Elements of Riding   **40**
    Go with Control the Movement   **40**
    Flexion, Turning and Bending   **41**
    Mechanics of Downward Transitions   **46**
    Auxiliary Aids and Throughness   **47**

Putting It All Together   **50**
    Exercises Designed to Tune Horse
    and Rider to Each Other   **50**
    Horse Characteristics   **52**
    The Training Scale   **54**

Acknowledgements

My deepest gratitude must first go first to all of the horses I have ridden and trained. Horses always speak the truth regardless of whether or not you want to know it. They truly live in the moment and learning to both listen and to speak to them nonverbally through body language has been an inspiring lifelong process.

To Barbara Christopher, my student and former textbook editor, I am in deep debt. This manual just simply would not exist without her encouragement and ability to help me organize many of my thoughts.

Learning to communicate effectively and subtly with horses through body language takes knowledge, practice and skill and I am grateful to have had some masters teach me. First, my appreciation goes to my late husband, Maj. Hector Carmona, who was a riding master in the Chilean cavalry, an Olympic modern pentathlon competitor representing Chile, a dressage judge and later coach for the United States Equestrian Team. It was Hector who taught me much of the basics of dressage. Following his death, I was fortunate to clinic with many wonderful trainers and instructors both in the USA as well as Europe.

Each one brought new dimensions with them. I owe an especially huge thank you to Alex Chterba from Russia and his wife, Vera Byalobzheskaya, who translated for us. Alex was a riding master in the Soviet Union and coached Olympian Nina Menkova and her mount, Dixon. He and Vera lived at my farm, Los Alamos Dressage Center, for about 2 years and I was fortunate to learn from him on a nearly daily basis. Alex was an especially gifted trainer of high collection (piaffe and passage.)

A huge thank you goes to all of my students, both past and present, who taught me to see and understand their issues. They made me think deeply about many aspects of riding which I had sometimes just taken for granted.

I am especially indebted to Christian Simonson and Katarina Antens-Miller for providing many photographs for this manual. Christian started to learn about dressage with me as an eight year old and became one of the top FEI junior and young riders in the USA as he continued to aspire to even higher goals. Katarina, a native of Sweden, studied with me for years and became a USDF Gold medalist. She has continued to train horses and riders. Others who contributed photos are Louise Lampara, Kristi Troyna , Shannon Peters and Frances Carbonnel. Thanks to all.

To those who did peer review for me, I am most appreciative. Noteworthy for their comments are dressage trainers/instructors Ann James and Shannon Peters, one of western dressage founders, Joyce Swanson, FEI "O" dressage judge, Janet Foy and former Olympian and USET technical advisor/Chef d'Equipe, Robert Dover. Many thanks.

Introduction

Harmonic Dressage® is a method of training both horse and rider in order to get the most out of the classical *Training Scale*. It strives to improve and refine nonverbal communication between horse and rider. As that communication develops, a partnership is formed based upon mutual trust and understanding between the two species. In harmony, they learn to communicate with each other almost effortlessly. That harmonious communication then allows horse and rider to perform as if of just one mind.

This manual, which consists of three parts, is designed to lay out basic elements important first in the education of the rider and second in the training of the horse. Good training of a horse requires understanding and ability on the part of a rider. First and foremost, the rider must learn how to sit and use the aids correctly. Riders should learn to communicate clearly to the horse so that the horse learns exactly what the rider means when applying a particular set of aids. In order to achieve these goals, a rider must first be trained how and what to communicate to the horse. This is a process that seemingly never ends since each horse is different from others and, although the principles remain the same, how they are applied might vary somewhat between horses. Nevertheless, a rider who wishes to ride and train a horse in dressage must learn some basic elements.

A Word About Dressage

Dressage, a French word that means training, is a rational and systematic method of training horses. The goal of it is to develop a horse into an athlete that is strong, calm, supple, loose and flexible while also remaining confident, attentive and able to respond rapidly to the aids of a rider.

Statue at Cavalry School, Chile

Dressage was developed over the centuries largely though cavalries as a clear and precise method of training designed to make horses easier to ride and better able to carry the weight of a person with less fatigue. Since it is a precise method based upon the biomechanics and psychology of the horse, soldiers who learned dressage could mount and easily ride a horse which had lost its rider in battle. Today, although cavalries have been disbanded, dressage methodology is still practiced the world over.

Terry Miller Photo

Author and Serr Maariner Working in Harmony

As a horse progresses in its training, the results will be reflected in greater freedom and regularity of its gaits. Movements requested of the horse will be achieved with lightness and harmony as well as energy and expression because the horse will learn to carry more weight behind, thus lifting the forehand and creating an uphill balance, generated by lively impulsion. Horses will learn to accept the bit and become submissive without tension or resistance. Thus, the horse will give the impression of doing of its own accord what is required by the rider.

Through learning subtle aids from the rider, horses become more obedient but yet very responsive to those aids. Creating better balance, straightness and relaxation in the body of the horse through correct dressage training produces more strength and flexibility in the horse's body. All of these factors help to protect the horse from premature aging, swaying of the back and injuries caused by overloading one part of the horse's body due to crookedness. When done well, horse and rider appear to be just one being doing movements in balance and of one mind or accord.

Over time, dressage has evolved into a science, an art and a sport all rolled into one. The science of dressage is represented in what is known as the *Training Scale* or *Training Pyramid*. The art of it resides largely in the ability of the educated rider to communicate quietly and effectively with the horse and the sport of dressage, now governed by the Federation Equestre Internationale (FEI), finds its pinnacle in Grand Prix at the Olympic Games.

Competitive dressage is composed of levels. It begins with easy exercises at the low levels and gradually increases in difficulty as the horse progresses up the levels. The exercises are introduced in a specific order so that the horse is appropriately prepared to do more difficult work before it is actually asked to do it. Each country has its own lower-level tests but the higher-level tests are international and are governed by the FEI. The FEI levels start at what is called Prix St. Georges and culminate at the highest Grand Prix level.

Photo Courtesy of Frances Carbonnel

Western Dressage Jog

In the first part of the 21st century, western dressage was born in the United States. It is also based upon the classical training scale but with focus upon training a horse to be suitable for working cattle and other western disciplines such as reining. Hence, the gaits (walk, trot and canter) of classical dressage changed to walk, jog and lope. These gaits show less impulsion (air time in the moment of suspension within a gait) but more efficiency since a western horse needs to become very agile and quick. Whereas classical dressage trains horses to achieve more *uphill* balance with great expression due to increased impulsion, western dressage horses develop more elasticity within their gaits and yet remain more earth bound as compared to classical dressage horses, a necessity for a western horse needing to look a cow in the eye and quickly maneuver it. Western dressage became a sport under the direction of the Western Dressage Association of America and it continues to evolve.

A Word About The Author

For almost as long as I can remember, I have had a very strong affinity for horses.

Author, age 4

At the age of two, my father bought a small Shetland pony stallion, Blackie. Blackie and I grew up together and were inseparable. Blackie was as strong willed as he was strong.

From him I learned to anticipate what he was going to do and prepare myself. In a sense, this was my first foray into dressage. In dressage, the rider must learn to listen to what the horse is saying with its body, learn to interpret the horse's body language appropriately and respond accordingly.

As I grew older, I hunted for a book from which I could learn how to train my pony and horses. Eventually someone gave me *Horsemanship*, a book by Austrian riding master and judge, Waldemar Seunig. As I read that book, I found myself underlining many sentences that I felt important and I started to gain a little insight into the classical method of training horses: dressage. I came to realize that I was fascinated with dressage even though I did not understand everything the author stated. It is now my desire to attempt to create a brief manual that lays out the principles of dressage in a way that is brief, concise and easy to follow.

I began my journey by breeding Arabian horses and trying to learn dressage from books. Dressage was very new to the United States and there were very few instructors available to me when I was a young adult. Eventually I met Maj. Hector Carmona, a retired cavalry officer from Chile, who had competed in the South American and Pan American Games, World Championships and the Olympic Games as a member of Chile's Modern Pentathlon team. He had also served as coach for the US equestrian team when the dressage team won the Silver

Maj. Hector Carmona Chilean Cavalry Riding Master

Medal and the Three-Day Event team won the gold in 1967 at the Pan Am Games. It was Hector who implanted the basics of dressage in my body and mind. I later married and worked with him to build Los Alamos Dressage Center, the first school of dressage in the United States. Eventually we imported some young Swedish Warmblood horses from Sweden.

After Hector's death in 1987, I changed my breeding program from Arabian to Swedish Warmblood horses and continued to pursue further education in dressage both in Europe as well as in the United States. At the same time, I was privileged to be able to breed and create a line of Swedish Warmblood horses which became known as the L.A. Baltic line. They became very successful not only in dressage sport horse breeding classes but also as competitors up through the highest levels both in dressage and hunters/jumpers.

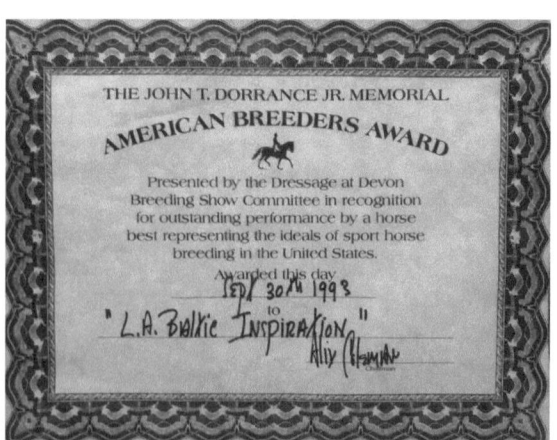

Throughout my life I have worked to develop a very educated eye. I am now able to equate what I can see and feel when I ride with what I know about biomechanics, psychology and the classic *Training Scale* of the horse. Thus, it is my intention to share some of my experience and education that I have learned over a lifetime. Although this manual is not intended to replace riding lessons, my hope is that it can serve as a guide for both riders and trainers.

I have not discovered any new principles of dressage, but I have a background and experience that are a bit unique and have allowed me to see the principles of dressage through the combined eyes of a trainer, horse breeder, competitor, clinician, coach and dressage judge. In addition to being a Ph.D. scientist, I am a USEF S Dressage, R Dressage Sport Horse Breeding and R Western Dressage judge.

I am also a USDF bronze, silver and gold medalist who has trained several horses through Grand Prix and coached several students to the same levels - some of whom have become professional dressage trainers. Based upon a lifetime of acquiring knowledge and experience, I am pleased to create a practical manual that can serve as a guide for riders of all disciplines who seek to use dressage methods to train their horses.

The Role of the Rider

Rider Requirements

In order to be able to ride a trained horse, it is important for the rider to gain sufficient knowledge of: 1) How to control their own body, 2) How and when to apply which aids, 3) How to control their own emotions and 4) How to be a good communicator – neither a self-absorbed dictator nor a passive passenger.

Independent Seat and Legs

In order to communicate quietly and effectively with a horse, a rider must develop a balanced seat in order to go with the movement of the horse as well as to influence the rhythm and tempo of the gaits. This requires a rider to develop an independent seat in which the two sit bones (ischial tuberosity) are centered over the backbone of the horse with both sit bones equidistant from the center of the horse's backbone. The lower back of the rider swings according to the movement of the horse. As the lower back swings in harmony with the movement of the horse, effectively separating the rider's upper body from their lower, the upper body appears to stay quiet and still relative to the movement of the horse and the seat of the rider stays in the saddle without bouncing.

Because of the structural pelvic differences between men and women, men sit on their two sit bones with their tail bone (last vertebra) pointed towards the back bone of the horse whereas women sit on a tripod between their 2 sit bones and their pubic bone. (Fig 1) These structural differences allow women to sit a little lighter on the back of the horse but they also give men the advantage of having a more engaged driving seat.

Claudia Craig photo

Fig. 1
Showing Differences Between Seat of Female **(L)** and Male **(R)** Riders
Photos Courtesy of FEI level riders, Shannon Peters **(L)** and Christian Simonson **(R)**

The Dressage Seat

Riders unfamiliar with this position will probably need to consciously learn how to relax their hip joints so that their legs can slide back from the hip. The ability of a rider to communicate effectively and subtly through body language with a horse will never be better than the ability of the rider to sit balanced on the horse without gripping. This is called an independent seat.

The Role of the Seat and Legs

Humans are very hand-eye oriented. We usually attempt to solve problems first visually and then by using our hands. However, the reins, which connect to the bit in the horse's mouth, should not be used by riders to try to shorten the neck of the horse, hold the head of the horse in one particular position nor to stop or slow the tempo of a gait. Instead, a rider needs to learn to use their seat and legs to control tempo, prepare transitions and keep the back of the horse up by connecting it to the bit. To develop an independent seat, the rider must control tempo and direction of movement with their seat and legs and create transitions between and within the gaits. Those requirements are best left up to instructors who know how to safely lunge riders without the use of stirrups or reins on trained horses that can be lunged in side reins. In side reins that are not too long nor too short, a horse will round and lift its back. When the back is round, a rider is then able to sit comfortably and do gymnastic exercises designed to help them find better balance and develop an independent seat.

Upper Body

Photo Courtesy of Christian Simonson

Fig. 2
Correct Body Alignment
The legs should lie gently against the rib cage of the horse. The legs should be in contact with the rib cage of the horse but should not grip the sides of the horse. The knees should be pointed down towards the ground and the lower leg pulled back slightly so that if a vertical line were drawn from the shoulder to the ground, it would pass through the head, shoulder, hip and heel of the rider.

As shown in Fig 3, the shoulders and arms of the rider must remain relaxed and quiet so that the rider's hands do not constantly move relative to the movement of the horse and do not create any jerky contact with the mouth of the horse. The upper body remains straight and appears to be quiet even as the horse moves. Shoulders should be relaxed but with shoulder blades flattened so that the arms hang down toward the ground and the elbows are bent at the waist. The wrists of the rider should be straight. The hand should be relaxed but with a closed fist and the thumb should be the highest point on the fist. This requires a supple back on the part of both the horse and the rider because half of the seat belongs to the rider and half is due to the horse lifting and rounding its back.

Photo Courtesy of Christian Simonson

Fig. 3
Correct Body Position

Lower Back

The rider's lower back must be able to swing in the same rhythm and tempo as the gait of the horse in order for the rider to remain seated and not bounce on the back of the horse. It is the responsibility of the rider to put equal weight on both sit bones and not to lean in any direction that would allow one sit bone to be weighted more than the other. The rider should not have to use the reins in order to keep their own balance. As mentioned previously, the swing in the rider's lower back separates the upper body from the lower body so that the lower body can sit quietly and comfortably upon the back of the horse and the upper body can remain still relative to the movement of the horse. At the same time, the horse must be taught to lift and round its back which will then offer a comfortable place for the rider to sit. If the horse has a stiff or hollow back, it will be difficult for a rider to sit comfortably.

For a rider to sit correctly, as outlined above, the rider must keep the horse connected over its back through half halts and downward transitions. When the horse's back is rounded, it is strong and can swing comfortably. If the back is hollow, it is weak, stiff and uncomfortable to sit on. Likewise, if a rider feels a horse pushing them to one side because of crookedness, the rider needs to apply the appropriate aids to push the horse's back under both of their two sit bones so that the back bone of the horse becomes centered between the two sit bones of the rider. Hence, a correct seat is achieved not only by the rider sitting correctly, but also by the rider keeping the horse's back round and in alignment.

One way to check to see if your alignment is correct is to ask yourself this question: If my horse suddenly evaporated under me, would I land on my feet? (Figs 4 and 5) If the answer is yes, then you are correctly aligned. If you feel as though you might land on your nose, you are leaning too forward and if you feel as though you would land on your buttocks, you are leaning too far back. If you are not feeling the back of your horse relaxed and easy to sit on, the most probable reason is that the horse's neck is either too high or too short or both. To have the horse round its back more, the rider should allow the horse to lower its neck in order to stretch in down and lengthen it enough to create a round back. When the back of the horse is round, the rider will be able to sit comfortably upon it.

a. b. c. *Photos Courtesy of Kristi Troyna*

Fig. 4
Rider Positions **a.** Leaning Back, **b.** Straight **c.** Leaning Forward

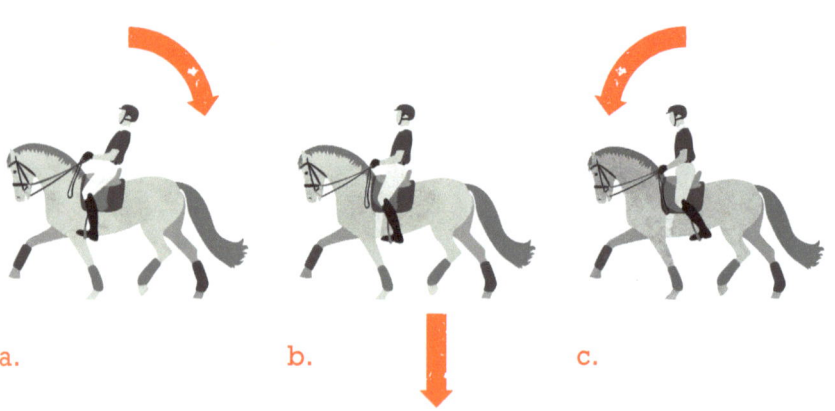

a. b. c.

Fig. 5
Arrows Show Direction of Balance of Rider
Rider Positions **a.** Leaning Back, **b.** Straight **c.** Leaning Forward

Co-ordinating the Seat and Legs with the Hands

Getting a Horse in Front of the Driving Aids

In order for both horse and rider to be comfortable and to perform efficiently, the horse must be taught to be responsive to light aids of the rider. In order to do this, the horse must first learn to move forward immediately from minimal driving aids. Upward transitions, such as walk to trot, should be repeated until the horse eagerly moves forward from very light leg pressure.

To ask a horse to move forward, the rider should start with minimal contact with the bit and apply small pressure with the calves of the legs behind the girth and engage the seat slightly by tilting the pelvis slightly forward. This can be accomplished when a rider simply contracts their gluteal muscles a little and points their belly button in the direction they wish to go, which, in this case, means to push the belly button forward. The rider's lower legs should press gently against the rib cage of the horse at the same time the pelvis is slightly tilted. The legs of the rider should not grip or get tight as that will inhibit the horse from moving forward.

Horses are not born knowing what leg pressure on their rib cage means. Likewise, horses are not born knowing what pressure from a bit in their mouth means. They need to be carefully taught what each aid means. With horses just being backed, it is advantageous to first teach the horse to move forward on a lunge line from the ground in order to teach them to move forward when a lunge whip is waved toward their hindquarters. If the horse does not move forward promptly when a rider asks for an upward transition, an assistant with a lunge whip can be helpful to teach the horse to understand the driving aids of the rider. With horses that are already broken, a sharper aid such as a kick, spur or touch with a whip should be used immediately after asking the horse to move forward if the horse is unresponsive. This exercise should be repeated until the horse understands to promptly move forward from very minimal leg and seat aids. When applying a sharper aid, always start by using it gently and only increase the pressure if the horse does not respond to a very light aid.

Keep the legs pressing gently for a few seconds until you feel the horse starting to move forward. As soon as the horse moves forward, relax the legs. Don't just kick with your leg or take it off too rapidly because such aids that are too rapid are meaningless to a horse. On the other hand, if the horse has not responded and started to move forward in about 3 - 5 seconds, the rider should follow up by the use a sharper aid such as the touch of the whip or spur to make it clear to the horse that it must immediately move forward.

A Word About Delay Time

There is a delay time between asking the horse to move forward and the horse actually moving forward. That delay time varies according to the sensitivity of both horse and rider as well as the ability of the rider to be clear with their aids. The reason is that the rider first must think that they want the horse to move forward and then that thought has to be translated into an aid, such as pressing with the legs. Next, the horse must feel the aid being given, and that sensation must go to its brain and be recognized as a request to move forward. Then the horse needs to translate the thought to move forward into actually moving forward. Finally, the rider must feel the horse moving forward, and that sensation must pass to the brain of the rider and be recognized as forward movement. All of that requires some finite period of time. It might take only a couple of seconds, but remember that the horse does not read your mind. The horse does not know that you want it to move forward until you communicate with your body and it receives that information in its brain. Only then can the horse respond. Delay time can be decreased through clear and repetitive practice as both horse and rider understand each other better and the horse becomes more sensitive to the aids.

Fig. 6

Visualization to Start Forward Movement

To ask a horse to move forward, imagine that the horse is a big balloon filled with air. Slide your legs back to embrace the barrel of the horse, and without raising your heels, imagine that your legs have wrapped around the barrel of the horse and that you are going to press gently with your heels on the belly button on the midline of the horse's belly. At the same time, use your seat and legs to press imagined air behind you up into the head of the horse. Gently press with your lower legs (be sure not to squeeze with your thighs or knees) and push your belly button out in front of you.

The Role of the Hands

The hands are receivers of the energy generated by the driving aids. In order to have the horse lift and round its back, riders must keep their fists closed and arms still relative to the movement of the horse. Then, when the horse is taking contact with the bit, it can yield at the poll, relax its jaw and lift and round its back. As the horse lifts it back, it will automatically transfer more carrying power into its hindquarters and create a relative lifting of the forehand. On the other hand, riders who try to create contact with the bit by pulling the head of the horse in and rounding the neck too much while also allowing the horse move forward, will slow the activity in the hind legs of the horse. This will create tension in the back of the horse, stiffness through its body and actually prevent the horse from rounding its back. More weight will be put on the forehand of the horse, making it more difficult for the horse to carry a rider's weight efficiently.

Connecting a horse from back to front requires that the rider must keep the hind legs of the horse very active and wait for the horse to connect with the hands of the rider, yield in the jaw and round its back. The horse must have the desire to move forward in balance with a rounded back. A horse that is pushed too hard by the rider will grab onto the bit and simply brace against it while trying to rush forward with a stiff or hollow back.

Rein aids regulate the forward driving aids and are applied by increasing or decreasing tension in the reins. The effectiveness of the rein aids depends largely upon the suppleness of the horse. Only a supple horse can willingly allow the influence of the reins to pass readily through the poll, neck, back and hind quarters.

The Four Rein Aids

1. Yielding Rein: This giving rein is the softest of the four rein aids. It can vary in extent from just more relaxation of the fingers to actually extending the arm more forward when lengthening of the neck of the horse is desired. The reins may actually slip through the fingers a little while maintaining contact or, if the horse is reluctant to stretch its neck down and out a little, the rider might have to actually drop the reins.

2. Light Contact: The degree of pressure in the horse's mouth is determined by the horse. Some horses prefer a heavier feeling on the bit but most prefer very light positive pressure. Contact should not be created by the rider actively doing anything with their hands. Contact is a result of connection created by the rider pushing the horse up into a receiving hand. When the horse is in good balance and self-carriage, the rider simply follows its mouth with a light contact.

If the horse begins to lose balance and fall onto its forehand, then pressure will be put on the hands of the rider and the rider will know that a half halt is needed in order to recreate good balance.

3. Half Halting or Non-Allowing Rein: With this rein aid, instead of following, the hand is steady and remains steady as the rider applies more driving aids until the horse submits in the lower jaw and becomes light in the hand. As soon as the horse submits, it is of the utmost importance that the rider immediately relaxes his/her arms to allow self-carriage. If the horse is through (willingly accepting the driving and receiving aids) when it is pushed against this steady hand, its frame closes from behind so it carries more weight on its hind legs. This half halt creates a more uphill frame and makes the horse lighter.

4. Supporting or Framing Rein: When bending a horse, the inside rein together with the hips, seat and leg of the rider create bend which is then controlled by the outside rein and leg of the rider. The outside rein becomes the supporting or framing rein and must be balanced against the inside rein. Too much outside rein can prevent the horse from flexing and bending while too little allows the outside shoulder of the horse to fall to the outside. When moving straight ahead the outside rein prevents the horse from over flexing to the inside at the poll and supports balance and straightness.

Contact and Connection

Once the horse is in front of the driving aids and responds quickly to light pressure from the seat and leg, the rider can then create a connection over the back of the horse. The connection is similar to a bridge that connects the hindquarters of the horse to the forehand. Connection is what causes the horse to lift and round its back. This is what makes the back of the horse strong and supple so that is can carry the weight of the rider more efficiently and also stay sounder and more flexible with age.

Photo Courtesy of Kristi Troyna

Fig. 7
Relaxation of Lower Jaw and Yield at Poll

To create this connection, a horse must first learn to relax its lower jaw and yield at the poll. (Fig. 7) One way to do that is at the halt. The rider can squeeze one fist to put pressure on one rein until the horse relaxes its lower jaw and yields at the poll. As soon as the horse responds, the rider must immediately relax their fist and repeat the process first on one side and then the other until the horse relaxes both sides of its jaw with its mouth closed.

Half Halts

Half halts are rider aids that are used to rebalance and alert a horse to a possible transition. Half halts are the moments when a rider speaks to the horse. In between them, the rider should be quiet and listening to the horse. These are the aids which, when applied correctly with correct timing, create the appearance of horse and rider to be of just one being doing movements in balance and of one mind or accord.

When walking or trotting, the rider can then use the seat and legs to push the horse up into contact with the bit. This is accomplished through half halts. When the horse feels pressure on its mouth, and if the rider insures that the horse's <u>hind legs stay active</u>, it will know to relax the lower jaw and yield at the poll in order to relieve the pressure created by the bit. As the horse yields to the pressure created by <u>pushing it forward into a quiet hand</u>, the horse will lift and round its back. As soon as this happens, the rider must relax his/her shoulders, arms and fists without moving them or opening the fingers. In order for them not to move, relaxation is done isometrically. In this way, the horse's movement and head carriage are not restricted by the hands of the rider and the horse is allowed to carry its own head while, at the same time, maintaining a soft feeling through the reins with the hands of the rider. The degree of connection will vary depending upon what the rider is asking for as well as the ability of the horse according to its level of training. (Fig. 8)

Photo Courtesy of Christian Simonson   *Photo Courtesy of Katarina Antens-Miller*

Fig. 8

Degree of Connection (and Collection) Varies with Level of Training of Horse. Lower Level Horse Taking Contact and Lifting Back **(L)** Upper Level Horse Taking Contact and Lifting Back with More Engagement **(R)**

To learn how do half halts correctly, riders need to first learn how to perform downward transitions, such as walk to halt or trot to walk, without the use of their hands. In general, to perform a downward transition, the rider should contract the gluteal muscles and sit a little taller by lifting the abdominal muscles for 1 or maximum, 2 steps. In so doing, the lower back of the rider will stiffen slightly so that the lower back will swing slightly slower than that of the horse. At the same time, the lower legs of the rider should lie gently against the rib cage of the horse in order to ensure that the horse maintains a light contact with the bit. The rider must use his/her legs or a light touch with a whip at the moment of the half halt to ensure that the hind legs of the horse remain active or even slightly more active. Rather than slowing down, the horse should engage its hindquarters more, compress its body and lift the forehand. It is very important that the rider not sustain the half halt aids for more than 1 or 2 steps because it they do, both the rider and horse will become stiff and instead of creating a better connection and better balance, the opposite will occur. Half halts can and should be repeated frequently in order to maintain good balance and awareness.

One effective method for riders to learn how to do half halts is to count steps. To start, a rider could do 10 steps of trot or jog followed by 10 steps of walk. Riders must use their seat and legs as described above to prepare downward transitions without stopping or slowing the horse with the reins. By counting steps, riders learn when to start and how frequently half halts must be done to create the exact number of steps, maintain a steady tempo and make smooth transitions with the horse connected to the bit but without actively pulling on the reins. Once horse and rider can perform smooth and balanced upward and downward transitions, riders should then decrease the number of walk steps between trot sets. Starting with 10 trot steps and 5 walk steps, riders should think about trotting as soon as they walk and think about walking as soon as they trot so that the transitions are simply allowed by the rider rather than suddenly created by the rider. To learn and practice quicker timing, decrease the number of walk steps gradually until the horse almost walks and maintains an active hind leg when only 1 step of walk is asked. When riders learn to do this well, they will have mastered the half halt at the trot.

Half Halts in the Canter

Half halts in the canter are performed at the moment of suspension when all four feet of the horse are off of the ground. The rider simply uses the aids to create slightly longer "air time." One method to help riders better understand the timing and the aids is to try to canter just 1 step nearly on the same spot and then immediately move on. To do so, the horse must take more weight behind, stay active in the hind legs and become more engaged. In the event that the horse tries to stop or get slow in the hind legs, a gentle tap with the whip will help to keep the hind legs active and thus increase the connection and collection of the horse.

Riding from half halt to half halt is the secret of balanced and harmonious riding. Whenever a rider feels the need to correct, rebalance, or bend the horse the rider should always start by doing a half halt and never start by pulling on the reins. In other words, riders should ride their horses up to the bit and not backwards from the hand.

Creating Connection over the Back of the Horse

It is extremely important to remember that the *connection* over the back of the horse must be created by <u>increasing activity in the hind limbs so that the horse pushes itself up to contact with the bit and creates a positive tension with the bit.</u> As the horse becomes more active in the hind legs and connects with the bit, its back becomes rounder and stronger. This is sometimes called "riding from the back to the front." <u>The horse should be the one who determines how much pressure is put onto the bit, not the rider.</u> Riders who flex and shorten the neck of the horse by pulling on the reins and/or keeping them too short create stiffness over the back of the horse. This scenario is sometimes called riding from front to back. Fig 9 illustrates correct and incorrect connection. A stiff back is not only uncomfortable to sit upon but that stiffness is also reflected in the quality and freedom of the gaits. Exercises designed to help both a horse and rider to better create a connection from the back to the front are discussed in Harmonic Dressage Part 3.

Photos Courtesy of Katarina Antens-Miller

Fig. 9

Riding from "Back to Front" (L) versus Riding "Front to Back" (R) Correct Connection with Increased Activity in Hind Legs and Horse Seeking Contact (L) versus Stiffness and Decreased Activity in Hind Legs with Poll Low and Neck Shortened (R)

Basic Elements of Riding

Go with and Control the Movement

Courtesy of Christian Simonson

Riders must learn to have control over their own bodies before they can hope to communicate clearly and effectively with a horse.

As mentioned previously, the lower back of the rider must swing back and forth comfortably. This will allow the seat to be steady with equal weight on both sit bones. The pelvis should not be allowed to swing from side to side because that will change the body's weight distribution with each stride. Shoulders and arms should be relaxed with shoulders flattened and elbows bent in order for the hands to remain steady relative to the movement of the horse. When the rider maintains correct position, his/her hands will remain steady even if a horse loses balance and falls against the hands of the rider. In such a case, the core and back of the rider will counterbalance the increased pressure exerted by the horse and the hand will remain passive. In other words, if a horse should lose balance and put 10 lbs. of pressure on the hands of the rider, the rider should not pull back but, by bracing with his/her body, counterbalance passively with just 10 lbs. (Not 9 lbs. nor 11 lbs.) As soon as the horse regains better balance, the rider should immediately relax his/her arm and allow the horse to return to self-carriage. Riders who round their shoulders or lengthen their arms by opening the elbows will never be able to respond in a timely or appropriate manner.

Flexion, Turning and Bending

Turning a horse is similar to steering a boat (from the rear) rather than a bicycle (from the front.)

Riders who try to turn a horse simply by pulling on the inside rein can create bend in the horse's neck, but the body of the horse will not follow the same bend. On the other hand, if the rider directs the hindquarters of the horse, the forehand, neck and head will all be pushed in the same direction.

Flexion: When traveling to the left, a horse is normally brought into left flexion by the rider and when traveling to the right, it is brought into right flexion. Flexions teach the horse to travel with the hind legs closer together which then creates more engagement and straightness through the body of the horse. When a horse is in left flexion, the left hind leg will step up toward the center of the belly of the horse in between the 2 front legs and the horse will flex slightly to the left at the poll. Flexion at the poll should occur only between the skull (atlas) and the first cervical vertebra (axis.) The neck of the horse should not be bent when the horse is moving straight ahead and the rider should not try to hold the head of the horse in any particular position. However, when a horse is in correct left flexion, for instance, the rider will feel the left hind leg well engaged and feel a little stronger contact on the right rein. This is often referred to as riding from inside leg to outside rein. At the same time, the rider will feel the lower jaw of the horse very relaxed

10a 10b 10c

Photos Courtesy of Louise Lampara

Fig. 10
10a Straight Horse – Hind Legs Directly Behind Front Legs and Neck Centered Between Shoulders 10b Horse in Left Flexion – Left Hind Leg Between 2 Front Legs, Flexed Left Only at Poll 10c Horse in Left Flexion Behind and at Poll but with Neck too Bent to the Left

and the contact will become so light that the rider will only notice the horse putting a light positive pressure on the reins (slightly more on the outside rein than the inside rein) due to forward impulsion and self-carriage as the horse establishes contact and straightens. (Fig. 10)

Turning: A horse should be turned primarily by the rider turning their hips, seat and legs to direct the hindquarters of the horse. The inside hand can be used to create flexion at the poll, as described above, while the outside hand prevents the horse's neck from bending. The neck of the horse should not be bent and should stay centered between its shoulders.

To change direction, a rider needs to keep their sit bones centered over the backbone of the horse and not lift either sit bone by leaning in one direction or the other. To turn the horse, the rider should sit deeply in the saddle and move the hips of the horse laterally by turning their own hips. The hips can easily be turned by directing the belly button in the desired direction. If the hips of the horse to not follow the hips of the rider, then tapping the inside hind leg of the horse with a whip will encourage that leg to step under the body and help the horse to turn.

Applying some pressure to the direct rein (rein that places tension on the bit and moves the horse's head toward the direction in which it is required to move) may also be necessary to direct the horse. If the direct rein (inside rein) is used, it is important to keep the indirect rein (outside rein) against the outside of the horse's neck to prevent the neck from bending. The neck of the horse should stay centered between its shoulder blades.

Bending: Actual bending of the horse occurs in the loin area (Sacro-lumbar area,) behind the saddle. If the neck is bent, for example to the left, the right shoulder will be pushed to the right and the horse will lean onto the left shoulder. Bending this way makes a horse "crooked" and pushes the horse to the outside (right in this case.) Both reins should be kept the same length by the rider preventing themselves from moving one arm back and the other arm forward. When both reins are kept the same length, the inside, direct rein will create flexion at the poll of the horse and push the horse toward the outside. When that happens, the outside, indirect rein, will receive the energy and keep the neck centered between both shoulders so that the horse is able to keep the outside shoulder on the circumference of a circle or on a straight line when moving straight ahead. (Fig 11)

The outside leg and outside rein of the rider should frame the horse. They prevent the hindquarters and outside shoulder from swinging to the outside when the rider applies inside aids to turn. The inside leg of the rider should remain slightly behind the girth and it acts like a post, allowing the horse to bend but also preventing it from leaning in. When the horse is bent correctly, the inside hind leg of the horse will become more engaged and travel up toward the center of the belly of the horse and the horse will be pushed up against the outside rein and leg of the rider. The rider must then set boundaries (frame the horse) by having the horse yield in its outside jaw and straighten so that the outside shoulder does not push to the outside. Likewise, the outside leg of the rider prevents the hindquarters from swinging to the outside. The horse will bend its body in the loin area and the hind legs of the horse will track up into the same tracks as the front legs. The neck of the horse will stay centered between its shoulder blades. (Fig 10) Turning a horse by turning the neck and hoping that the hindquarters will follow not only unbalances the horse but also creates crookedness in its body.

Photo Courtesy of Katarina Antens-Miller

Fig. 11
Correct Bending
Neck of Horse Centered Between Shoulder Blades Hind Feet Step Into Same Tracks as Front Feet

Mechanics of Downward Transitions

Transitions are very important because through them the horse becomes trained to understand the aids of the rider. Transitions create better balance and promote more sensitivity and communication between horse and rider. Transitions occur between gaits (such as walk-halt-walk or trot-halt or walk-trot etc.) and within gaits (such as a collected trot-extended trot-collected trot, etc.) Downward transitions, especially, are key to creating collection.

To avoid stiffening of the back of the horse in a downward transition, such as trot to halt or extended trot to collected trot, the rider should avoid pulling on the reins, or worse, by leaning back and pulling on the reins. Instead, half halts are used to get the attention of the horse and prepare it for a movement, such as a transition, by creating a better connection over the back of the horse. Repeated movements will create downward transitions without creating tension over the back of the horse. Sometimes, especially with a very forward moving horse, the rider will also need to apply a little pressure around their knee area.

As the horse comes to the halt, the rider's lower legs need to apply light pressure. This will keep the hindquarters engaged. As the horse is pushed up to the bit as it halts, the body of the horse is compressed with the back well rounded due to engagement of the hindquarters. In the halt, the horse should be balanced and ready to move immediately forward from a rider's light seat and leg pressure. If the horse does not engage the hindquarters well and round its back in the halt, the rider can tap the hindquarters with a whip in the transition to halt.

If a horse gets onto its forehand, half halts will help to rebalance it. When that occurs, the rider should not pull back on the reins nor relieve the pressure by opening the hand and losing the connection. Instead, the rider should create more activity in the hind legs of the horse (a whip can be helpful if the horse tries to stop or slow the hind legs) which will cause the horse to further engage the hind quarters and round the back. That will transfer weight from the forehand onto the hindquarters.

Auxiliary Aids and Throughness

In addition to the seat, legs and hands, riders may at times need the use of one or more of the auxiliary aids. The spur and/or whip can be very useful tools to make the meaning of a leg aid emphatic and clear if a horse does not respond appropriately to leg aids. The spur should only be used on an "educated" leg that is quiet and relaxed along the side of the horse without having the toes turned out. Riders should not constantly have their spurs in contact with the sides of the horse. They can apply the spur when the horse does not respond well to pressure from their legs. The spur or whip will create a brief but more intense aid to help to create a better connection over the back of the horse. In general, the axillary aids are used to enhance the sensitivity of the horse to forward movement and increased activity in the hind legs.

As the energy lines in Fig 12 show, the whip or spur is used to energize the hindquarters of the horse and to push the back of the horse upward and into the legs of the rider. The rider's legs bring the energy of the horse onto the bit and from the bit through the reins into the rider's hands. From the hands, the circle continues through the seat of the rider onto the horse's back, finally to return to the hind legs, where the circle closes and the whole process begins anew. When the horse responds to the aids of the rider without resistance, it is said to be through, which is essential for impulsion.

The circle of aids coincides with the horse's ring of muscles, which was discovered roughly 100 years ago by two German veterinarians, Doctors Simon and Haase. They found that a horse's fine balance between the ability to bend and the ability to stretch can be attributed to the undisturbed flow of energy through the muscle ring. As the muscles of a horse work in a ring pattern from the poll over the hindquarters and the belly; back to the chest into the jaw, so do the aids of the rider.

The whip or spur's job is to awaken the horse's sensitivity and create more activity in the hind quarters. The horse must learn to understand that a light tap of the riding whip means "flex the joints in the hindquarters and immediately move forward." Hence, the whip is used in the circle of aids to put the horse in front of the driving aids of the rider.

Author, Gail Hoff

Fig. 12
The Circle of Aids Showing Energy Lines

Putting it All Together

Exercises Designed to Tune Horse and Rider to each other

Just as every day is a new day, every ride is a new ride. Both horse and/or rider may be either dull or sharp, stiff or loose, relaxed or tense and comfortable or uncomfortable in varying degrees. Consequently, it is wise for a rider to start the ride by showing the horse how they use their seat and aids that ride and at the same time the rider must learn the horse's response.

After allowing the horse to walk, trot and canter on a relatively loose rein to relax and loosen its muscles, transitions are the key to start to tune horse and rider to each other. First, the rider should be sure that the horse is in front of the driving aids and that it will move forward eagerly and promptly when very light seat/leg aids are applied.

Starting with walk-halt-walk transitions, the rider should repeat these transitions as many times as necessary until the horse responds quickly and willingly to very light seat/leg aids of rider and makes downward transitions with hind legs engaged, mouth closed and without shortening the neck.

Next, walk-trot-walk transitions will start to refine the communication process between horse and rider. The rider should plan when and/or where the transitions will be made far in advance of doing them. This can be done by deciding upon how many steps of each gait should be made or at what marker in the arena the transition should be made. Such planning will help the rider to fine tune their own aids so that instead of suddenly asking for a transition, the rider will use small half halts to prepare the horse for a transition and then simply allow it.

Trot-halt-trot transitions including trot-halt-rein back-trot transitions will help to further balance the horse and sensitize it to the stronger transitions. Likewise, Canter-halt-canter and canter-halt-rein back-canter transitions will help to create more thoroughness. Transitions within the gaits such as working or medium-extended-collected-medium etc. will further refine the communication channels between horse and rider.

Once the horse and rider are really tuned to each other, the rider will have helped the horse to find what I like to call the zone of all possibilities. This zone is reflected in the ability of the horse to nearly effortlessly perform any gait or transition in good balance and without hesitation.
Transitions are the key to training a horse.

Horse Characteristics

Although there are many variations, horses have stronger and weaker conformation points which makes training them by a specific methodology more or less difficult. The skill and knowledge of the rider as well as the conformation, ability and talents of the horse all work together in the training process.

Every horse will improve its balance, gaits and sensitivity when trained by dressage methodology.

Some breeds have been selected for a specific purpose and their conformation will usually reflect that purpose. For instance, the American Quarter Horse was bred to work cattle and its downhill conformation (croup higher than withers) allows it to easily adjust its body so that it can look a cow in the eye. On the other hand, European warmbloods have been bred largely for the sports of dressage, jumping and three-day eventing which are more easily performed on a horse that has an uphill (croup lower or equal to height at withers) conformation. Thus, when applying dressage methods to training very different kinds of horses, the results will reflect not only the training method but also the ability, conformation and desired job of the horse.

Although some horses are selected and trained with dressage techniques for the sport of dressage, there are some general principles that apply to any horse undergoing training. The first requirement should be that the horse is healthy and sound as determined by a veterinarian. Secondly, any horse should learn to be both mentally and physically relaxed. These are prerequisites which make training any horse easier and more fruitful. Several books and trainers who specialize in teaching such prerequisites are available and it is beyond the scope of this manual to address such methods.

The Training Scale

Collection *Versammlung*	Increased Engagement, Lightness of forehand, Self-Carriage)	
Straightness *Geraderichtung*	Improved Alignment and Balance	
Impulsion *Schwung*	Increased Energy and Thrust	
Connection or Contact *Anlehnung*	Acceptance of the Bit through Acceptance of the Aids	
Suppleness *Losgelassenheit*	Elasticity and Relaxation	
Rhythm and Regularity *Takt*	With Energy and Tempo	

What sets dressage training apart from other types of training is what has become known as the *Training Scale* or *Training Pyramid*. It is a systematic method for training horses which builds on the capabilities and training of the horse starting with a horse just beginning its life as a riding horse to one which is trained up through the highest levels.

Dressage is like the ballet or gymnastics of the horse world. It teaches the horse to become stronger, more flexible, better coordinated and able to perform intricate movements with grace and calm. There is no end to it because every horse is different and there is always something new to learn.

Harmonic Dressage® Manuals

Harmonic Dressage® Part 1, Optimizing Your Seat and Use of the Aids addresses rider mechanics and techniques

Harmonic Dressage® Part 2, Techniques of Harmonic Dressage Training addresses understanding the Training Scale and the purpose of various movements

Harmonic Dressage® Part 3, Methodology of Harmonic Dressage

Index

aids, 8, 9, 10, 17, 22, 25, 26, 27, 28, 30, 31, 32, 33, 34, 37, 38, 44, 46, 47, 48, 49, 50, 51.
See rider auxiliary, *See* spur, *See* whip.
driving, 26, 33
    light aids, 25
    rein, 31
        direct, 43
        half halting or non allowing, 32
        indirect, 44
        inside, 44
        light contact, 31
        outside, 44
        support or framing, 32
        yielding, 31

bending, 32, 43, 44

C

communicate, 5, 8, 10, 17, 19, 27, 40, *See* move forward: delay time

connection
> riding from the back to front. *See* horse connected over its back crookedness, 10, 22, 45
>
> crooked, 44

D

dressage, 5, 6, 7, 8, 9, 10, 11, 13, 14, 15, 16, 52, 53, 56
> goal of, 9
>
> levels, 10
>
> science, an art and a sport, 10
>
> western, 11

F

Federation Equestre Internationale (FEI), 10

flexion, 3, 41, 42
> at the poll, 42
>
> Fig 10, 42

hind legs closer together, 41

inside leg to outside rein, 42

half halts, 22, 34, 37, 38, 46, 47, 51
- canter, 38
- rebalance, 34
- relax lower jaw and yield at the poll, 34
- rider speaks to the horse, 34

Harmonic Dressage, 8, 40, 56, 57
- methodology, 57
- seat and use of the aids, 57
- techniques of, 57

Harmonic Dressage®, 56, 57

horse, 8, 9, 10, 11, 13, 14, 15, 17, 18, 19, 20, 21, 22, 23, 25, 26, 27, 28, 30, 31, 32, 33, 34, 36, 37, 38, 39, 40, 41, 42, 43, 44, 45, 46, 47, 48, 49, 50, 51, 52, 53, 56
- breeds, 52
- conformation, 52
- through, 48
- horse connected over its back. *See* rider:correct body alignment:horse's back round
- connection, 33, 39
- degree of connection, 36

engage hindquarters, 37
hind legs of the horse very active, 30
horse lift and round its back, 30
relative lifting of forehand, 30

Maj. Hector Carmona, 13
move forward, 25, 26, 27, 30, 49, 50
    delay time, 27
    Fig 6 visualization to start forward movement, 29
    from minimal driving aids, 25
    on a lunge line, 26

reins, 19, 20, 22, 31, 36, 38, 39, 43, 44, 46, 47, 48
    side reins, 20
rider, 8, 9, 10, 13, 17, 18, 19, 20, 21, 22, 23, 25, 26, 27, 28, 30, 31, 32, 33, 34, 36, 37, 38, 39, 40, 41, 42, 43, 44, 45, 46, 47, 48, 49, 50, 51, 52, 57, *See* move forward
    balanced seat, 17
    correct body alignment, 20

horse's back round, 23
one way to check, 23
hand-eye oriented, 19
hands
    receivers, 30
hands, 21
hands
    isometrically, 36
hip joints, 19
independent seat, 17, 19, 20
keep horse connected, 22
    half halts and downward transitions, 22
lower back, 17
    separates the upper body from the lower body, 22
    swing in the same rhythm and tempo as gait, 22
seat and legs
    control tempo, 19
    create transitions, 19
shoulders and arms, 21
sit bones (ischial tuberosity), 17
    equal weight, 22
upper body, 18, 21
wrists, 21

S

self-carriage, 31, 32, 41
sit bones (ischial tuberosity). See rider
spur, 26, 27, 47, 48, 49
supple back
    horse, 21
    rider, 21

T

Training Scale, 3, 8, 10, 15, 54, 56, 57
transitions, 19, 22, 25, 37, 38, 46, 50, 51
    downward, 37
    upward, 25
turn, 43, 44
turning, 43, 45

W

Western Dressage Association, 11
whip, 26, 27, 37, 39, 43, 47, 48, 49

zone of all possibilities, 51

www.ingramcontent.com/pod-product-compliance
Lightning Source LLC
Chambersburg PA
CBHW040002110526
44587CB00001BA/31